CW00382066

THE WAY OF THE CROSS WITH SAINT PAUL

By the same author and published by ST PAULS:

A Shoot from the Stock of Jesse
A Time to Seek the Lord
Mary, Woman of Prayer
The Greatest of These is Love

The Way of the Cross with Saint Paul

Bishop Michael Campbell OSA

ST PAULS

Scripture passages translated from the Greek by the author.

Illustrations by Francis Teague

Cover picture: *St Paul Writing* by Paul Francesco Saachi, © National Gallery, London.

Published by ST PAULS Publishing, London SW11 3AS
Copyright © ST PAULS, London, 2009

ISBN 978-0-85439-754-9

Set by Tukan DTP, Stubbington, Fareham UK
Printed by AGAM, Cuneo, Italy.

ST PAULS is an activity of the priests and brothers
of the Society of St Paul who proclaim the Gospel
through the media of social communication.

CONTENTS

INTRODUCTION

The cross of Jesus Christ held a central place in the thought and teaching of the Apostle Paul. Christ's offering of himself as a sacrifice on the cross was for Paul the turning point in human history. At the heart of the Apostle's preaching was the reconciliation of humanity to God which the Son of God accomplished by his obedience unto death on Calvary. The references to the cross and its redemptive power in Paul's writings are numerous, and the mystery of God's love manifested there clearly left the most profound impression on him.

The Stations of the Cross are a much loved devotion in the Catholic Church, particularly so during the season of Lent. In this year, devoted to the memory of the great Apostle, the Church invites us to ponder Paul's life and teaching, and on the perennial value of that teaching. These meditations on our Lord's sufferings, the 'Way of the Cross', draw their inspiration from the letters of Saint Paul. With him as guide, our understanding and appreciation of our Lord's sufferings can only be immeasurably enhanced.

+Michael Campbell OSA

Let us ask St Paul to obtain for us
the grace of making the Way of the Cross well.
St Paul is the great preacher of "Jesus crucified".
In his letter to the Corinthians (1 Cor 2:2) he wrote
*'For I decided to know nothing among
you except Jesus Christ, and him crucified'*.
May he stir up those same feelings in us.

THE WAY OF THE CROSS

V. We adore you, O Christ, and we bless you.

R. Because by your holy cross you have redeemed
the world.

PRAYER

Look down, O Lord, on this your family, for whose sake
our Lord Jesus Christ did not hesitate to give himself up
into the hands of the wicked and to suffer the torments
of the cross. You who live and reign for ever and ever.
Amen.

ACT OF CONTRITION

My most merciful Jesus, humbly prostrate at your most
holy feet, with all my heart I ask pardon for my sins,
which I deplore and detest because they are an offence
against your infinite goodness. I resolve to die rather
than offend you again; and I resolve to love you above all
things until death.

V. Have mercy on us, O Lord.

R. Have mercy on us.

Our Father...

Jesus is condemned to death

V.   We adore you, O Christ and we bless you.

R.   Because by your holy cross you have redeemed the world.

*... Christ Jesus, who made the
good confession of faith before
Pontius Pilate*

1 Timothy 6:13

The cross of Jesus Christ lies at the heart of Paul's Gospel. From the moment of his conversion on the road to Damascus, and for the rest of his life, the death of the Lord by crucifixion was a source of unending wonder to him. Paul came to realise that while Pontius Pilate may have passed the sentence of death humanly speaking, the true reason for the cross was to be found instead in the immense love of Jesus Christ for the world. The knowledge of Christ's cross has changed everything. Against those who would devalue Christ's death, Paul remarks "*The life I live now is a life of faith in the Son of God, who loved me and gave himself for me*" (Gal 2:20).

Paul spent his life as an apostle proclaiming that Christ's death on the cross marked the end of the old order and the beginning of a new creation. We know that he suffered greatly for the sake of the gospel, but what sustained him was the presence of Christ who was crucified in weakness and raised to glory by the Father's power. When trials and difficulties come our way, let us draw comfort from Paul's words, "*Therefore I am content with weaknesses, insults, difficulties, persecutions, troubles, for the sake of Christ. For when I am weak, it is then that I am strong."* (2 Cor 12:10).

PRAYER

Lord Jesus Christ, by your silence you gave eloquent witness as you were condemned to death on the cross by Pontius Pilate. After the example of your great apostle, Paul, may we place all our trust in your cross, the enduring sign of your unending love for us and for the world; You who are God, living and reigning for ever and ever. Amen.

V. Have mercy on us, O Lord.
R. Have mercy on us.

Our Father…

At the cross her station keeping,
Stood the mournful Mother weeping
Close to Jesus to the last.

Stabat Mater dolorosa
Juxta crucem lacrimosa,
Dum pendebat Filius.

Jesus embraces his cross

V. We adore you, O Christ and we bless you.

R. Because by your holy cross you have redeemed the world.

God forbid that I should glory except in the cross of our Lord Jesus Christ, through whom the world is crucified to me and I to the world.

Galatians 6:14

For the world of Paul's day, the cross was a symbol of contempt, humiliation and weakness. Yet for Paul it was different. For the Apostle, the cross was the place where the power of God was most dramatically at work. Far from being ashamed of the cross of Christ, Paul's faith allowed him to boast of it, and even to identify himself with Christ hanging on the cross. "*With Christ, I have been crucified*" (Gal 2:19). The crucified Christ would prove a stumbling-block to those who did not believe, but to the eye of faith the same Christ demonstrated the power and the wisdom of God.

Death and resurrection were a constant theme of Paul's preaching. Our first encounter with the cross of Christ took place in our baptism, when in a profound if mysterious way we died and were buried with Christ in order to share his risen life. The Apostle teaches that as disciples of Christ we must constantly relive the reality of our baptism through dying to selfishness and embracing the new life which the risen Lord offers us.

PRAYER

Lord Jesus, through the power of your grace may we glory in your cross, through which we are crucified to the world and the world to us. Let us never shirk from the way of the cross, a way which you have already travelled and made the source of our salvation. We make this prayer through Christ our Lord. Amen.

V. Have mercy on us, O Lord.
R. Have mercy on us.

Our Father…

Through her heart, His sorrow sharing,
All His bitter anguish bearing,
Now at length the sword had passed.

Cujus animam gementem,
Contristatam et dolentem,
Pertransivit gladius.

Jesus falls the first time

V. We adore you, O Christ and we bless you.

R. Because by your holy cross you have redeemed the world.

Recognise the grace of Our Lord Jesus Christ: although he was rich, he became poor for your sake, so that through his poverty you might become rich.

2 Corinthians 8:9

The helplessness of Christ on his way to Calvary reflects the depth of his self-emptying, as Paul describes the Incarnation, when he assumed the condition of a slave and became obedient to death, even death on a cross (Phil 2:8). Paul sees this supreme act of obedience of Christ as sharply contrasting with the wilful disobedience of Adam, our first parent. Adam's deed brought sin and death to humanity; Christ's offering of himself on the cross brought redemption and life to a countless multitude.

The Apostle often refers in his letters to the 'mystery of Christ', at the heart of which is the cross. Only love can shed light and help explain the sufferings willingly undertaken by the Son of God for our sake. With Saint Paul, we too can only marvel at what Christ has accomplished through his cross, pondering the mystery prayerfully and silently.

PRAYER

Lord Jesus, in obedience to your Father, you walked the way of the cross in frailty and pain. When we encounter difficulties in life, let us draw inspiration from your apostle Paul who contemplated your cross and so found strength in weakness. You who live and reign for ever and ever, Amen.

V. Have mercy on us, O Lord.
R. Have mercy on us.

Our Father…

Oh, how sad and sore distressed
Was that Mother highly blessed
Of the sole-begotten One!

O quam tristis et afflicta
Fuit illa benedicta
Mater Unigeniti!

Jesus meets his mother

V. We adore you, O Christ and we bless you.

R. Because by your holy cross you have redeemed the world.

Now I am glad to be suffering for you, and so make up in my body what is lacking in the sufferings of Christ for his body, the Church.

Colossians 1:22

As the first disciple of Christ, his mother Mary exemplified in a unique way the truth enunciated by Paul that, in a manner we don't fully understand, our personal sufferings benefit the wider Church, which Paul calls the body of Christ. Mary gave birth to Christ and remained faithful to him, sharing his sufferings as she stood at the foot of the cross. As we contemplate the meeting of mother and Son we are reminded of the Apostle's teaching, especially applicable in Our Lady's case, that in order to claim her share of Christ's glory, she had first to share in her Son's sufferings, (Rom 8:17). The Virgin Mary can truly claim, with Paul, to have fought the good fight of faith and to have run her race to the finish.

We look on Our Lady as a mother and teacher, and Paul's words can be fittingly applied to Mary, *Imitate me, as I imitate Christ* (1 Cor 11:1). The Mother of the Lord and Saint Paul form part of that first community of disciples whose teaching and example in the face of adversity instruct and encourage us on our pilgrim way to God's kingdom. Their witness to the truth of Jesus Christ was unshakeable, a witness made even more resplendent by their own individual participation in his passion.

PRAYER

Lord Jesus, your mother Mary and the apostle Paul as your faithful disciples shared in your sufferings and left us a witness of faithful endurance. We pray that we can embrace our sufferings with faith and unite them with your passion and death for the salvation of the world. You who are God, and live and reign for ever and ever. Amen.

V. Have mercy on us, O Lord.
R. Have mercy on us.

Our Father…

Christ above in torment hangs,
She beneath beholds the pangs
Of her dying, glorious Son.

Quae moerebat et dolebat,
Pia Mater, dum videbat
Nati poenas inclyti.

Simon of Cyrene helps Jesus to carry his cross

V. We adore you, O Christ and we bless you.

R. Because by your holy cross you have redeemed the world.

Carry one another's burdens,
and so you will fulfil the law of Christ.

Galatians 6:2

Paul reflects almost to the letter the teaching of Christ in the gospels that the whole Law can be summed up in the command to love our neighbour as ourselves (Rom 13:8-10). Just as Christ carried his cross to Calvary, assisted by Simon from Cyrene, Paul, using the same language, exhorts his converts to carry one another's burdens if they are to live as Christ taught. We see here what a faithful witness Paul was to the tradition of Christ as he found it in the early Church. This concern of the Apostle for fellow Christians suffering want and deprivation finds practical expression in his desire that collections be taken up on their behalf (Gal 2:10; 2 Cor cc8-9).

By shouldering the cross of Christ, Simon could be described as the perfect embodiment of the Good Samaritan in the parable spoken by Christ. Paul, in his own way, fulfilled the role of a Good Samaritan and true friend to those Gentiles who had never heard of Christ. Only the overwhelming love of Christ (2 Cor 5:14), could impel Paul to proclaim the Christian gospel to the vast and unbelieving pagan world. It is when we are graced with insight into the extent of the crucified Christ's love for us that reaching out to our neighbour in Christian charity becomes less burdensome.

PRAYER

Lord Jesus, you graciously accepted the help of Simon on your path of suffering. Your apostle Paul urges us to carry one another's burdens along the road of life and so fulfil your law of love. Of ourselves we fall short, but through your grace all things are possible. You who live and reign for ever and ever. Amen.

V. Have mercy on us, O Lord.
R. Have mercy on us.

Our Father…

Is there one who would not weep
Whelmed in miseries so deep
Christ's dear Mother to behold?

Quis est homo qui non fleret,
Matrem Christi si videret,
In tanto supplicio?

Veronica wipes the face of Jesus

V. We adore you, O Christ and we bless you.

R. Because by your holy cross you have redeemed the world.

*These women worked together with me
in preaching the gospel…
their names are recorded in the book of life.*

Philippians 4:3

On his extensive missionary journeys Paul was grateful for the welcome and hospitality extended to him, (e.g. Acts 18:1-11; Rom 16:1-16) and he showed particular appreciation to the community at Philippi for the gifts they sent him. The Apostle's spectacular achievements in spreading the gospel of Christ in the face of considerable opposition of all kinds was undoubtedly due to the help and support of so many whose names are unrecorded. The tradition which has come down to us that Veronica wiped the face of our Lord on his journey to Calvary, stands as one example among many of those women and men who ministered to Christ in his need, and who later were so instrumental under God in the building up the early Church.

Paul reminds us that as believers we form the body of Christ, with each one of us having our own part to play in the building up of that body. The various gifts we have been graced with, whether ordinary or extraordinary, are given for the benefit of others. The kind gesture of Veronica, for ever remembered, stands as an example of the lasting importance of apparently little deeds.

PRAYER

Lord Jesus, you call us to be part of the community which is your Church. Your apostle Paul teaches us that you live in the heart of each one of us through the power of the Holy Spirit, and that we should make hospitality our special care. We pray that the Apostle's teaching may find expression in our manner of life. You who live and reign for ever and ever. Amen.

V. Have mercy on us, O Lord.
R. Have mercy on us.

Our Father...

Can the human heart refrain
From partaking in her pain,
In that Mother's pain untold?

Quis non posset contristari
Christi Matrem contemplari
Dolentem cum Filio?

Jesus falls the second time

V. We adore you, O Christ and we bless you.

R. Because by your holy cross you have redeemed the world.

God did not spare his own Son,
but gave him up for us all.

Romans 8:32

The weak Christ under the weight of his cross, but trusting completely in God his Father, struggled with difficulty to the place of execution. His willingness to embrace suffering would inspire Paul in his own trials and tribulations as an apostle. Paul never wavered in his conviction that the power of God was most powerfully present when the challenges confronting him appeared to be overwhelming. He remarks, *For we live always, given over to death for Jesus' sake, so that the life of Jesus may be manifest in our mortal flesh* (2 Cor 4:11).

The Apostle could even rejoice in what he had to suffer in his work of proclaiming the gospel, for he knew that Christ had already triumphed over all evil and adversity through his cross and death. Moreover, he had the assurance of faith that the trials of this present life are short lived, and are but a prelude to the glory that awaits us with the risen Christ.

PRAYER

Lord Jesus, you shared in our human nature and can sympathise with us in our weakness. In imitation of Saint Paul give us courage and faith when crosses come our way, for you will not allow us to be tempted beyond our strength. You who live and reign for ever and ever. Amen.

V. Have mercy on us, O Lord.
R. Have mercy on us.

Our Father…

Bruised, derided, cursed, defiled,
She beheld her tender Child,
All with bloody scourges rent.

Pro peccatis suae gentis
Vidit Jesum in tormentis,
Et flagellis subditum.

The women of Jerusalem weep for our Lord

V. We adore you, O Christ and we bless you.

R. Because by your holy cross you have redeemed the world.

Rejoice with those who rejoice,
weep with those who weep.

Romans 12:15

The women of Jerusalem were moved with compassion for Christ as he made his sorrowful way to Calvary. Through their compassion they shared in his sufferings. A feature of Paul's apostolic ministry was his sense of identity with others, irrespective of their race, creed, or social class. *Although a free man, I became a slave to gain as many as I could; and to the Jews I became as a Jew so as to win over as many as possible; to those not under the Law I became as not under the Law… so as to win over those not under the Law; to those who were weak I became weak, so that I might win over the weak. I became everything to everyone, so that I may win at least some of them* (1 Cor 9:19-22). The love of Christ overcame all barriers.

The women of Jerusalem defied the opposition and hostility of the Roman soldiers to show their sympathy for Christ. The apostle Paul spared no effort and faced many dangers in bringing the healing word of Christ's gospel to the Gentile peoples. He has left us a fine example of Christian courage. May we never be ashamed to witness to the gospel of Christ to the men and women of our world.

PRAYER

Lord Jesus, you graciously acknowledged the tears of the women of Jerusalem as you carried your cross. Your apostle Paul exhorts us to make our own the joys and sorrows of others. Whatever our own trials, give us the generosity of spirit to recognise the needs of others. You who live and reign for ever and ever. Amen.

V. Have mercy on us, O Lord.
R. Have mercy on us.

   Our Father…

   For the sins of His own nation
   Saw Him hang in desolation
   Till His spirit forth He sent.

   Vidit suum dulcem Natum
   Moriendo desolatum,
   Dum emisit spiritum.

Jesus falls the third time

V. We adore you, O Christ and we bless you.
R. Because by your holy cross you have redeemed the world.

Christ loved the Church
and gave himself up for her.

Ephesians 5:25

In his reflection on the great drama of the incarnation, death and resurrection of Christ, Paul pointedly observes that the death in question was that of the cross, with all the humiliation and cruelty that such a death entailed (Phil 2:6-11). The fall of Christ for the third time shows the depths of the humiliation attached to the cross. Paul never ceased to be amazed at the love which drove Christ to such self-abasement. The love of Christ would henceforth prove to be the driving force and motivation for his life and work as an apostle.

For Paul, the cross of the Lord Jesus was an object of love and reverence, the sign of God's victory over sin and evil. His own spiritual life found expression and meaning in the language of the cross, for he taught that if we wish to live with Christ we must first die with him. That identification with the crucified Christ takes place in our baptism, *so that as he was raised from the dead by the Father's glory, we too might live a new life* (Rom 6:4).

PRAYER

Lord Jesus, you left your Father's side in glory and took up the cross to save us all. Let us take to heart the teaching of Saint Paul that through our baptism we are united with you in death, and now in faith share the glory of your risen life. You who live and reign for ever and ever. Amen.

V. Have mercy on us, O Lord.
R. Have mercy on us.

Our Father...

O thou Mother! fount of love,
Touch my spirit from above,
Make my heart with thine accord.

Eia Mater, fons amoris,
Me sentire vim doloris
Fac, ut tecum lugeam.

Jesus is stripped of his garments

V. We adore you, O Christ and we bless you.

R. Because by your holy cross you have redeemed the world.

Through the obedience of one man,
many will be made righteous.

Romans 5:19

The cruel humiliation inflicted upon Jesus, when he is stripped of his clothes at the place of crucifixion, brings to full circle the great drama that began in the eternity of God when he stripped himself of his divine nature and clothed himself in our humanity (Phil 2:6). Paul urges his converts to have the same mind as Christ, one of absolute self-abnegation, to put the interests of others before their own. A Christian community is called to imitate the example and love of Christ which was totally devoid of self-interest, and a love whose unfathomable depths were revealed on the cross.

To make uniquely our own the fruits of Christ's passion, the Apostle insists on the necessity of stripping off our old selves and being re-clothed in that self which has been made new in the image of our creator (Col 4:9-10). For those of us who belong to Christ, death and resurrection must be the hallmark of our lives. To speak of Christ without his cross would have been inconceivable for the great Apostle. In this he is at one with Christ himself who laid down the condition of the cross for those who would follow him.

PRAYER

Lord Jesus, by your humiliation you humbled earthly pride, and through your apostle Paul teach us that your divine power shines through our human weakness. Help us take to heart the lessons of your Passion so that we may know that peace which passes all understanding. You who live and reign for ever and ever. Amen.

V. Have mercy on us, O Lord.
R. Have mercy on us.

Our Father…

Make me feel as thou hast felt;
Make my soul to glow and melt
With the love of Christ, my Lord.

Fac ut ardeat cor meum
In amando Christum Deum,
Ut sibi complaceam.

Jesus is nailed to the cross

V. We adore you, O Christ and we bless you.

R. Because by your holy cross you have redeemed the world.

God forbid that I should glory except in the cross of our Lord Jesus Christ, through whom the world is crucified to me and I to the world.

Galatians 6:14

As Paul reflected on the physical torment which Christ endured through being nailed to the cross, he came to realise that the debt sinful humanity incurred because of sin was being simultaneously nailed to the cross with Christ. Through his own suffering Christ abolished that sentence hanging over us (Col 2:14). The generous love of the righteous one which knew no bounds caused many to be made righteous. Paul understood our sinful condition as being the result of disobedience. The wounds of the crucified and obedient Christ now bring radical healing to our helpless state.

The mystery of human suffering often marks and disfigures the world around us. The Apostle would encourage us to turn our gaze to the One who hung in agony on the cross for our sake, and to unite our sufferings with those of Christ. His sufferings embraced in love give meaning to ours. In patient endurance we find peace through the blood of his cross. Paul even boasted of his share in the cross, and bore its marks in his own body (Gal 6:16).

PRAYER

Lord Jesus, from your wounds flows the source of our healing. Upon the cross, you encircled us all with your outstretched arms and so reconciled us to your Father. In imitation of your apostle Paul may we patiently accept our share of the cross, for in that cross lies our hope and salvation. You who live and reign for ever and ever. Amen.

V. Have mercy on us, O Lord.
R. Have mercy on us.

Our Father…

Holy Mother, pierce me through,
In my heart each wound renew
Of my Saviour crucified.

Sancta Mater, istud agas,
Crucifixi fige plagas
Cordi meo valide.

Jesus dies on the cross

V. We adore you, O Christ and we bless you.

R. Because by your holy cross you have redeemed the world.

He humbled himself,
becoming obedient to death,
even death on a cross.

Philippians 2:8

The risen, glorified Lord whom Paul encountered on the road to Damascus, was the same Jesus who suffered death on the cross. Paul now knew his true identity, and realised that his death was no ordinary death, for he was put to death for our sins and raised to life for our justification (Rom 4:25). The cross of Christ marked the end of the reign of sin and death. The saving design of God for the human race was miraculously accomplished by the death of *the one who did not know sin, but whom God made into sin for our sakes, so that we might become in Christ the justice of God* (2 Cor 5:21).

For the people of the ancient world, death on a cross was shameful and contemptible. But for the apostle Paul, Christ's death on the cross represented the great turning point of history. The death of Jesus Christ reversed the old order in which sin and death held sway. Paul would preach to the Gentile world that salvation and freedom were now available through faith to every person because of the death of that one man. As we prayerfully contemplate Christ on the cross, may we draw the courage and inspiration for our own life and for the moment of our death when it comes to us.

PRAYER

Lord Jesus, impelled by love you suffered the death of the cross to bring peace and reconciliation to a troubled world. Your apostle Paul teaches us that through our baptism we have become one with you in death; by the grace of your cross may we die to sin and selfishness and come to experience the power of your risen life. You who live and reign for ever and ever. Amen.

V. Have mercy on us, O Lord.
R. Have mercy on us.

Our Father...

Let me share with thee His pain,
Who for all our sins was slain,
Who for me in torments died.

Tui Nati vulnerati,
Tam dignati pro me pati,
Poenas mecum divide.

Jesus is taken down from the cross

V. We adore you, O Christ and we bless you.

R. Because by your holy cross you have redeemed the world.

If we have died with him,
we shall also live with him.

2 Timothy 2:11

The body of the Lord Jesus now lies in death. Paul writes that Christ loved the Church and gave himself up for her (Eph 5, 25). The love which alone gives meaning to the cross of Christ is a love from which we can never be separated, in life or in death. Paul boldly and remarkably declares that God did not spare his own Son, but sacrificed himself for the sake of us all (Rom 8:32). For the Apostle, the self-surrender of Christ in death marked the supreme expression of God's love for the world. It was for this reason that Paul could even boast of the cross of our Lord Jesus Christ.

Of ourselves, we were helpless and unable to achieve righteousness before God. It was then that Christ came to our rescue, the just One for the unjust. Paul further reflects that if Christ's death had such profound consequences for us, what subsequent benefits will accrue to us through sharing his life as the Risen One! (Rom 8:10). None of us should henceforth ever feel alone or unloved. Christ, lying in death, speaks of a love beyond words.

PRAYER

Lord Jesus, through your death you broke the ancient power of sin and death, and through the shedding of your blood brought us the peace of heaven. Following the teaching of your apostle Paul, may we place all our faith in your saving cross and so come to the glory of your resurrection. You who live and reign for ever and ever. Amen.

V. Have mercy on us, O Lord.
R. Have mercy on us.

Our Father…

Let me mingle tears with thee,
Mourning Him Who mourned for me,
All the days that I may live.

Fac me tecum pie flere,
Crucifixo condolere,
Donec ego vixero.

FOURTEENTH STATION
Jesus is laid in the tomb

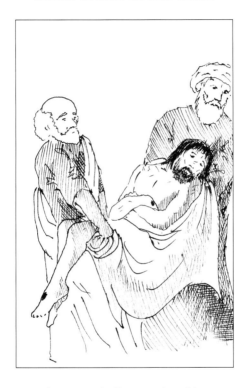

V. We adore you, O Christ and we bless you.
R. Because by your holy cross you have redeemed
the world.

I have handed on to you what I myself have received, namely that Christ died according to the Scriptures, that he was buried, and that he was raised to life on the third day...

1 Corinthians 15:3-4

The Lord Jesus has shared the common lot of humanity and entered the dark night of death. He is laid in the tomb. But he would not remain there and his burial was but a prelude to the glory of Easter Day. Yet Paul saw the Lord's death as full of consequences for all humanity, for Christ's death had broken the stranglehold of death exercised over the human race. By descending into the tomb, Christ has confronted and defeated the final enemy. The Apostle can ask triumphantly, *Death has been swallowed up in victory. Death, where is your victory? Death, where is your sting?* (1 Cor 15:55).

Paul would devote his apostolic life to preaching a crucified Christ, a Christ who died in weakness, yet the One in whom God was reconciling the world to himself (1 Cor 1:23). Death no longer held fear or terror for him or any of the other apostles, for Paul had the assurance that the crucified Jesus of Nazareth lay no longer imprisoned in death, but was now the Lord of glory, seated at the right hand of the Father. We firmly believe the testimony of Paul, which is that of the early Church, that the risen Christ is the firstborn of many brothers and sisters, and that he will in his own time transform our mortal bodies too into the likeness of his own glorious body (Phil 3:21).

PRAYER

Lord Jesus, you came into our world and laid down your life to restore a fallen humanity. Take from us the fear of death. Let us make our own the sentiments of your apostle Paul, that here on earth you are the source of our life, and passing through death we will see you face to face. You who live and reign for ever and ever. Amen.

V. Have mercy on us, O Lord.
R. Have mercy on us.

Our Father…

By the cross with thee to stay,
There with thee to weep and pray,
Is all I ask of thee to give.

Iuxta crucem tecum stare,
Et me tibi sociare
In planctu desidero.

The Resurrection of Christ from the dead

V. We adore you, O Christ and we bless you.

R. Because by your holy cross you have redeemed the world.

Now Christ has been raised from the dead, the first fruits of those who sleep; since through a man came death, through a man has also come the resurrection of the dead.

1 Corinthians 15:21-22

Since his conversion experience Paul's faith in Christ raised from the dead was unshakeable. He had met and spoken with Jesus. The world had irrevocably changed. Christ now reigned in glory with God his Father, and was the source of the life-giving Spirit of holiness poured out upon the world, into the hearts of those who believe. The old order had been reversed, even abolished. A new creation for those who believed in Christ had begun (2 Cor 5:17). The long-standing, ancient promises made by God to Abraham and the Fathers of the people of Israel had now come to pass when Christ rose in glory from the tomb. Paul staked his life and his credibility as a preacher of the gospel on Christ's resurrection (1 Cor 15:14).

With his profound insight into what he termed the 'mystery of Christ', Paul the theologian and teacher of the faith now became aware of how the glorified Christ, no longer confined within the constraints of time and space, was now present and active within the Church in every part of the world. Through the preaching of the Church and her sacraments, the risen Saviour meets afresh every generation with his word of life. He awaits each of us in faith to reveal himself to us, as he did to Paul on the road to Damascus, for he is in truth the One in whom the fullness of the godhead is to be found (Col 1:19).

PRAYER

Lord Jesus, your apostle Paul dwelt lovingly on the mystery of your cross and resurrection. We were once signed with your cross when we were baptised. We pray that its power may sustain us on our pilgrimage through life, and at the end bring us safely to share the glory of your resurrection. You who live and reign for ever and ever. Amen.

V. Have mercy on us, O Lord.
R. Have mercy on us.

Our Father...

While my body here decays,
May my soul Thy goodness praise,
Safe in paradise with Thee. Amen.

Quando corpus morietur,
Fac ut animae donetur
Paradisi gloria. Amen.

CLOSING PRAYER

Father, you have willed to save us through the death of Christ your Son on the cross. Grant that we who have known the mystery of his love here on earth may enjoy the fruits of his redemption in heaven. Through the same Christ our Lord. Amen.

– • –

According to the intentions of the Holy Father

Our Father, who art in heaven, hallowed be Thy name. Thy kingdom come, Thy will be done on earth, as it is in heaven. Give us this day our daily bread, and forgive us our trespasses, as we forgive those who trespass against us, and lead us not into temptation, but deliver us from evil. Amen.

Hail Mary, full of grace, the Lord is with thee, blessed art thou among women, and blessed is the fruit of thy womb, Jesus. Holy Mary, Mother of God, pray for us sinners, now, and at the hour of our death. Amen.

Glory be to the Father, and to the Son, and to the Holy Spirit; as it was in the beginning, is now, and ever shall be, world without end. Amen.

THE GIFT OF LOVE

If I speak in the tongues of mortals and of angels, but do not have love, I am a noisy gong or a clanging cymbal. And if I have prophetic powers, and understand all mysteries and all knowledge, and if I have all faith, so as to remove mountains, I am nothing. If I give away all my possessions, and if I hand over my body so that I may boast, but do not have love, I gain nothing.

Love is patient; love is kind; love is not envious or boastful or arrogant or rude. It does not insist on its own way; it is not irritable or resentful; it does not rejoice in wrongdoing, but rejoices in the truth. It bears all things, believes all things, hopes all things, endures all things.

Love never ends. But as for prophecies, they will come to an end; as for tongues, they will cease; as for knowledge, it will come to an end. For we know only in part, and we prophesy only in part; but when the complete comes, the partial will come to an end. When I was a child, I spoke like a child, I thought like a child, I reasoned like a child; when I became an adult, I put an end to childish ways. For now we see in a mirror, dimly, but then we will see face to face. Now I know only in part; then I will know fully, even as I have been fully known. And now faith, hope and love abide, these three; and the greatest of these is love.

1 Corinthians 13